Know About
Vinoba Bhave

KNOW ABOUT VINOBA BHAVE

ALL RIGHTS RESERVED. No part of this book may be reproduced in a retrieval system or transmitted in any form or by any means electronics, mechanical, photocopying, recording and or without permission of the publisher.

Published by

MAPLE PRESS PRIVATE LIMITED
office: A-63, Sector 58, Noida 201301, U.P., India
phone: +91 120 455 3581, 455 3583
email: info@maplepress.co.in
website: www.maplepress.co.in

Reprinted in 2019

ISBN: 978-93-50334-18-8

Contents

Preface 5
1. An Overview 6
2. Birth and Childhood 9
3. The Eccentric Vinoba 11
4. Meeting Gandhi 14
5. At Wardha 17
6. The Individual Satyagrahi 20
7. In Jail 24
8. The Spiritual Successor 26
9. Apostle of non-violence 30
10. The Padayatra 33
11. On Gita 37
12. On Education 41
13. On Hinduism 45
14. On Peace 48
15. On the Deed of Shanti Sena 52
16. On Cow Slaughter and Vegetarianism 57
17. Concept of Modern Society 61
18. On Planning 64
19. Vinoba's Message 66
20. On Political System 69
21. An Anecdote 72
22. Contemporaries of Vinoba 74
23. Jayprakash Narayan on Vinoba 78
24. Awards and Recognitions 81

Preface

Vinoba Bhave stands as a symbol of the struggle of the good against the evil, of the spiritual against the mundane. He was a spiritual visionary, whose spirituality had a pragmatic stance with intense concern for the deprived. He was a brilliant scholar, whose knowledge was accessible even to the ordinary people. He was Gandhiji's ardent follower, who could retain originality in thinking. As S. Radhakrishnan pointed out, "his life represents a harmonious blend of learning, spiritual perception and compassion for the lowly and the lost." His 'Bhoodan' (Gift of the Land) movement, which started on April 8, 1951, attracted the attention of the world. But, being untouched by publicity and attention, Vinoba continued his efforts for a just and equitable society.

This book deals with Vinoba Bhave, whose life is a saga of his commitment to non-violent ways of bringing changes, his yearning for the highest level of spirituality and his unwavering faith in human values and love.

CHAPTER 1
An Overview

Archarya Vinoba Bhave said, "It is a curious phenomena that God has made the hearts of the poor, rich and those of the rich, poor... What we should aim at is the creation of people power, which is opposed to the power of violence and is different from the coercive power of the state... A country should be defended not by arms, but by ethical behavior."

Acharya Vinoba Bhave was a scholar, saint, man of God, moral tribune, a beacon of hope and solace to millions in India and abroad. He was Mahatma Gandhi's spiritual successor.

Vinobaji, born in a village in Maharashtra, was drawn to Mahatma Gandhi and his unique 'Weaponless War' as a youth.

Like Mahatmaji, Vinobaji had also been much ahead of his time. His Bhoodan (Gift of Land), Sampattidan (Gift of Wealth), Jeevandan (Gift of Life) and other movements are logical extensions of Gandhiji's programme of national reconstruction.

Vinobaji was one of the greatest scholar-saints spawned by the modern Indian renaissance. His talks on the Bhagvad Gita, delivered in jail, are innovative and inspiring.

Though he had a marvellous memory and was a student by nature, he devoted the largest part of his time to spinning, in which he was specialised. He believed in universal spinning as the central activity, which would remove the poverty in the villages.

He abolished every trace of untouchability from his heart. He believed in communal amity. In order to know the best mind of Islam, he gave one year to the study of the Koran in the original. He, therefore, learnt Arabic. He found this study necessary for cultivating contact with the Muslims living in the neighbourhood.

The Padayatra (journey) of Vinobaji, which was part of his Bhoodan movement, now belongs to history. It was a demonstration of the Gandhian doctrine of Trusteeship.

Of the many teachings of the Gita, which Vinobaji highlighted in his talks, one of the most important was the role of self-help. "The Gita is prepared to go to the lowest, the weakest and the least cultured of men. And it goes to him not to keep him where he is, but to grasp him by the hand and lift him up. The Gita wishes that man should make his action pure and attain the highest state," said Vinoba.

No doubt, the nation has rightly honoured him posthumously with the Bharat Ratna Award, the highest civilian award for his service in 1984.

CHAPTER 2
Birth and Childhood

On September 11,1895, a son was born to the Vinobas, a Brahman family in the small village of Gagoda in Kolaba district of Maharashtra. This child, who was known as Vinayak in his early years, was no other than Acharya Vinoba Bhave. During his later years, he proved to be a great scholar and a beacon of hope and solace to millions in India and abroad. Many people even refer to him as the spiritual successor of Mahatma Gandhi. During his childhood, Vinayak was influenced by his mother Rukmini Devi, a religious woman.

The seeds of the benevolent Vinayak were sown early in his life by his mother. The Vinobas, like any rural household in those days had a huge orchard in their yard. The orchard had an abundance of different types of fruits. The child Vinayak was very fond of ripe fruits and he relished eating them whole. But, his mother always used to cut the fruits into pieces and say to him, "Distribute these fruits among village children and then you can eat it." Needless to say, this habit remained with Vinoba even in his later years.

Apart from these lessons at home, there were also other factors, which contributed to the formation of the character of the child Vinayak. Quite early in his life, Vinoba developed the habit of reading. During his school days, in Baroda, he read many biographies of great people; which inspired him throughout his life. Through his books, he came to understand the importance of sacrificing one's life for any noble cause. His hobbies during this time mainly included walking long distance with his friends, a habit which helped him in his later years during the famous Padayatra (foot march).

CHAPTER 3
The Eccentric Vinoba

Vinoba displayed leadership qualities quite early in his life. At the age of 19, in 1914, he and his friends formed the 'Vidyarthi Mandap' or student union. The friends of this Mandal, remained with him for his entire life. During the year of the formation of the Mandal, they together collected 1600 books for their school library.

Vinoba, who was well-read in the writings of Maharashtra's saints and philosophers at a young age, and deeply interested in Mathematics, was attracted to the core of learning. Naturally, the routine course of work was not enough to quench his thirst for knowledge.

Vinoba was very eccentric as a youth. For this reason, his two years in the college remained full of internal discomfort and disturbances. He did not have much faith in the education system of those times and, hence, he could not derive much from the formal training he got from his school and college days. Early in 1916, he put his school and college certificate in a fire on his way to Mumbai, in March 1916, to appear for the intermediate examination. He took a fateful decision not to go to Mumbai, but to go to 'Varanasi' (now called 'Benaras'). This decision was motivated by his longing to attain the eternal and all pervading Lord Brahma. He got into the study of the ancient Sanskrit test.

There was another incident, which took place during his early years, which further revealed his eccentricity.

One day, as Vinayak was returning home from school, he met his father's friend on the way. Vinayak was looking very shabby with un-shaved beard and uncombed hairs. His father's friend remarked, "Why don't you keep your hair organized?" Quickly came his reply, "I think you are a barber because only they observe people's hair." Needless to say, Vinayak received a deserving punishment. This incident had a lasting impression on Vinayak and he promised to change himself in the near future. And what a change it was! He is, probably, one of the most talked about leaders of modern India.

CHAPTER 4
Meeting Gandhi

It has already been mentioned in the previous chapter that Vinoba decided to go to the holy city of Benaras. He reached the city in 1916. But, soon, he began to think of his vocation in the future. He had two options in mind, first to go to the Himalayas and become a religious person, and the other to go to West Bengal and join the guerrillas fighting the British.

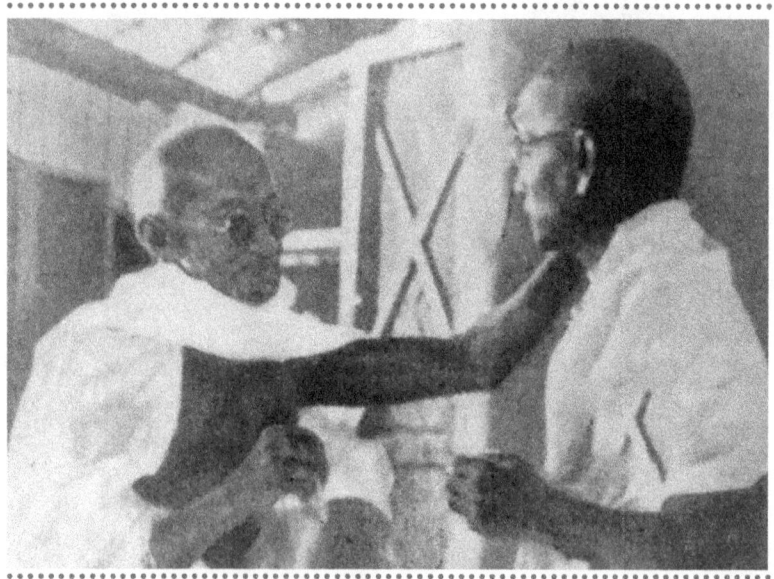

Just as he was contemplating about his future course of action, a report, in all the leading newspapers, caught his attention. It was about Gandhiji's speech at the newly founded Benaras Hindu University. This attracted Vinoba's attention. He was highly impressed by the contents of the speech. He decided to write a letter to Gandhiji. After an exchange of letters, Gandhiji finally advised Vinoba to come for a personal meeting at Kochrab Ashram, in Ahmedabad.

The meeting between the two legends was itself a historic event. On June 7, 1916, Vinoba went and met Gandhiji. Without doubt, this meeting changed the course of Vinoba's life.

Later, while describing the meeting Vinoba said, "When I was in Kashi, my main ambition was to go to the Himalayas. Also there was an inner longing to visit Bengal. But neither of the two dreams could be realised.

Providence took me to Gandhiji and I found in him not only the peace of The Himalayas but also the burning fervor of resolution, typical of Bengal. I said to myself that both of my desires had been fulfilled."

At the Gandhiji's ashram, Vinoba keenly participated within all its activities, like teaching, studying, spinning and working for the improvement of the community. Thus, Vinoba got involved in the life of Gandhiji, his spiritual Guru.

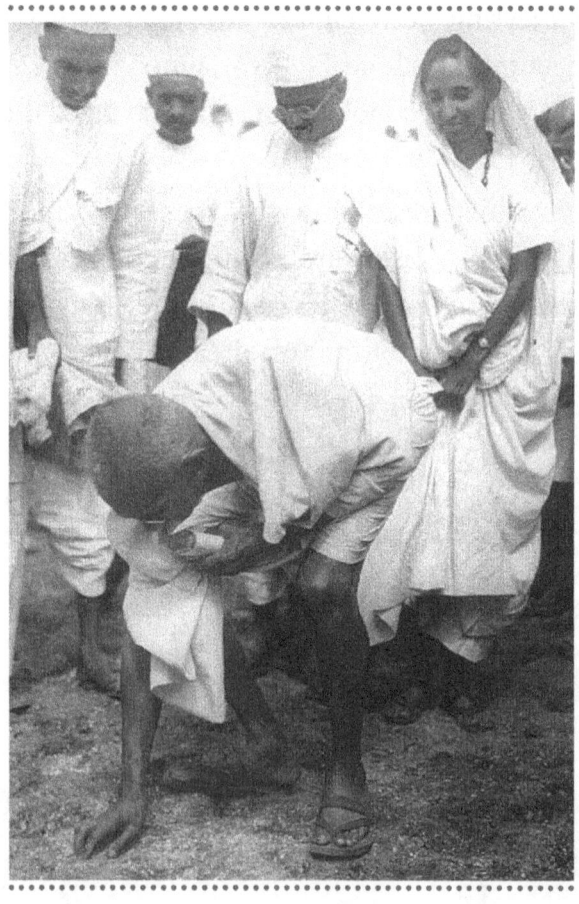

CHAPTER 5
At Wardha

Over the years, the bond between Vinoba and Gandhiji grew stronger.

There was an interesting incident that took place at Gandhiji's ashram, which shows his undying love for his Guru.

It was a custom in the ashram of Gandhiji to serve food in the dining hall. Most of the times, bitter gourd was served as the *sabji*, as it was cheap. Vinoba had a sweet tooth and he did not like bitter gourds. To get rid of the sabji as fast as he could, he would gulp them before carrying on with his meal. So, when Gandhiji came to serve the food, he found no *sabji* in his plate. Gandhiji was not aware of Vinoba's dislike for the vegetable, and on the contrary, he thought that Vinoba liked it very much, and thus he served him the *sabji* again and again. Later, Vinoba said that he started liking bitter gourd just because Gandhiji served him.

On April 8, 1921, Gandhiji asked Vinoba to take charge of the ashram in Wardha. Here, too, Vinoba devoted himself completely to the task of following the teachings of Sunday. In 1923, he brought out 'Maharashtra Dharma', a monthly in Marathi (regional language), which had his essays on the Upanishads. Later on, this monthly became a weekly and continued for three years. His articles on the Abhangas of Sant Tukaram (a saint poet) published in the weekly became popular. As time passed, Vinoba continued his search for the self, which took him to spiritual heights. His involvement with Gandhiji's constructive programs related to Khadi, village industries, new education (Nai Talim), sanitation and hygiene, also kept on increasing.

In December 23,1932, he shifted to Nalwadi (a village about two miles from Wardha town), from where he experimented his idea of supporting himself by spinning alone. Later, when he was sick in 1938, he shifted to what he called Paramdham Ashram in Paunar, which remained his headquarters.

Among the Gandhi's disciples, it was Vinoba who best appreciated the spiritual dimension of Gandhi's vision. He understood that Gandhi aimed at something greater than independence from Britain, His guru's dream was nothing less than the kingdom of God. While resistance had its place in the struggle, Gandhi believed that colonialism must also be uprooted from within. It was necessary to overcome the cultural and spiritual habits of dependence, fear and division that were the footholds of foreign oppression. That was the logic behind the spinning wheel.

Not only did the production of homespun cloth withdraw the market for imported British fabric, but also it affirmed social equality, simplicity, native culture, and the dignity of common labour.

CHAPTER 6
The Individual Satyagrahi

Apart from his involvement in the activities of Gandhiji's ashram, Vinoba also participated actively in the freedom movement during this period.

In 1923, he was jailed for months at Nagda jail and Akola jail, for taking a prominent part in the flag Satyagraha in Nagpur. In 1925, he was sent by Gandhiji to Vykon (in Kerala) to supervise the entry of the Harijans into the temple.

In 1932, he was jailed again for six months, in Dhulia, for raising his voice against the British rule.

He was selected as the first individual Satyagrahi by Gandhiji in 1940.

Vinoba was not known nationally when Gandhiji selected him for individual Satyagraha. Hence, Gandhiji had to issue a statement in the 'Harijan' on October 5, 1940, introducing Vinoba to the public:

"He is an undergraduate having left college after my return to India in 1916. He is a Sanskrit scholar. He joined the Ashram almost at its inception. He was among the first members. In order to better qualify himself, he took one year's leave to prosecute further studies in Sanskrit. And practically at the same hour at which he had left the Ashram a year before, he walked into it without notice. I had forgotten that he was due to arrive that day. He has taken part in every menial activity of the Ashram from scavenging to cooking. Though he has a marvellous memory and is a student by nature, he has devoted the largest part of his time to spinning in which he has specialised as very few have. He believes in universal spinning being the central activity, which will remove the poverty in the villages and put life into their deadness. Being a born teacher, he has been of the utmost assistance to Asha Devi in her development of the scheme of education through handicrafts. Sri Vinoba has produced a textbook taking spinning as the handicraft. It is original

in conception. He has made scoffers realize that spinning is the handicraft par excellence which lends itself to being effectively used for basic education.

For perfect spinning probably, he has no rival in all India.

He has abolished every trace of untouchability from his heart. He believes in communal unity with the same passion that I have. In order to know the best mind of Islam, he gave one year to the study of the Quran in the original. He therefore learnt Arabic. He found this study necessary for cultivating a living contact with the Muslims living in his neighbourhood."

"He has an army of disciples and workers who would rise to any sacrifice at his bidding. He is responsible for producing a young man who has dedicated himself to the service of lepers. Though an utter stranger to medicine, this worker has by a singular devotion mastered the method of treatment of lepers and he's now running several clinics for their care. Hundreds owe their cure to his labours. He has now published a handbook in Marathi for the treatment of lepers. Vinoba was from years the director of the Mahila Ashram (an ashram for women) in Wardha. His devotion to the cause of Daridranarayan (the God of the poor) took him first to a village near Wardha, from where he has established contact with villagers through the disciples he has trained.

He believes in the necessity of the political independence of India. He is an accurate student of history.

But he believes that real independence of the villagers is impossible without his constructive programme of which *khadi* is the centre. He believes that the *charkha* is the most equitable outward symbol of non-violence, which has become an integral part of his life. He has taken an active part in the previous Satyagrah campaigns. He has never been in the limelight on the political platform. With many co-workers he believes dead silent constructive work with civil disobedience in the background is far more effective than the already heavily crowded political platform. And he thoroughly believes that non- violent resistance is impossible without a heart belief in and practice of constructive work."

With this, the initiation of Vinoba as Gandhiji's successor was complete.

CHAPTER 7
In Jail

Throughout his life, Vinoba continued to be in the limelight of India's struggle for freedom.

During 1940-41, he was jailed thrice for individual Satyagraha at Nagpur jails, first time for three months, the second time for six months and third time for one year. Vinoba also took part in the Quit India movement of 1942, for which he got an imprisonment of three years at Vellore and Seoni jails.

Not being a one to take life in jail as a setback, Vinoba made the jail a place for fulfilling his favourite hobbies- reading and writing.

In the Dhulia jail, he began the proof reading of his book 'Gitai' (Marathi translation of Gita).

Vinoba also gave lectures on the Gita to his fellow prisoners in the Dhulia jail, which were later collected by Sane Guruji as a book.

His achievements during his life in the Nagpur jail include, writing of the book 'Swarajya Shastra' (the treatise of self-rule), and the collection of the bhajans (religious songs) of saints Gyaneshwar, Eknath and Namdev.

Vinoba wrote the *'Ishavasyavritti'* and *'Sthitaprajna Darshan'* during his stay in the Seoni jail.

In the Vellore jail, Vinoba, the knowledge seeker, learned four languages of South India. During this time, he also scripted the Lok Nagari after extensive research work. His writings covering diverse areas of religion, philosophy and education are thought-provoking, and yet accessible to the common people. The popularity of his writings has proved his ability to relate to the people. The competence of this multi lingual scholar as an editor was also of high order as displayed as the editor of 'Maharashtra Dharma', Sarvodaya (in Hindi) and Sevak (in Marathi).

Through his skill and agility, Vinoba changed the worst part of his life to the most productive years of his life.

CHAPTER 8
The Spiritual Successor

Soon after India's independence, came the news of Gandhi's assassination. Though grief-stricken, many of Gandhi's comrades felt by this time that the victory of independence was achieved. But Vinoba, Gandhiji's spiritual successor, vowed to carry forward the struggle for Gandhi's wider goal, Sarvodaya, a non-violent society dedicated to the welfare of all.

In March 1948, Gandhiji's followers and constructive workers met at Sevagram. The idea of Sarvodaya Samaj (society) surfaced and started getting acceptance. Vinoba got busy with activities, which aimed at soothing the wounds of the partition of the nation. In the beginning of 1950, he launched the programme of Kanchan-mukti (freedom from dependence on gold, i.e. money) and Rishi-Kheti (cultivation without the use of bullocks as was practised by Rishis, i.e, the sages of ancient times). In April 1951, after attending the Sarvodaya conference at Shivnampalli, he started his peace-trek on foot through the violence-torn region of Telangana (now in

Andhra Pradesh). The disturbances were caused by the communists residing in the state. On April 18, 1951, his meeting with the villagers at Pochampalli opened a new chapter in the history of non-violence struggle. The Harijans of the village told him that they needed 80 acres of land to make a living. Referring to this, Vinoba asked the villagers if they could do something to solve this problem. To everybody's surprise, Ram Chandra Reddy, a landlord, got up and showed his willingness to give 100 acres of land. This incident, unplanned and unheard, showed a way to solve the problem of the landless. The Bhoodan (Gift of the Land) movement was launched. The response to the movement was spontaneous. In Telangana, the gift of land averaged 200 acres of land per day. On the journey from Paunar to Delhi, the average gift was 300 acres a day. Vinoba had five crore acres as the target. While walking

in Uttar Pradesh, in May 1952, Vinoba received the gift of the whole village of Mangrath. This meant the people were prepared to give all their lands for the benefit of all the villagers, not as individual Bhoodan, but as community Gramdan (Gift of the Village).

Vinoba received land worth Rs. 23 lakh, in Bihar, while walking from September 1952 to December 1954. Orissa, Tamil Nadu and Kerala contributed significantly to Gramdan. Vinoba firmly believed, "We must establish the independent power of the people - this is to say, we must demonstrate a power opposed to the power of violence and other than the power to punish. The people are our God." Connected with Bhoodan and Gramdan, there were other programmes. Important of these were Sampatti-Dan (Gift of the Wealth), Shramdan (Gift of the Labour), Shanti Sena (Army for Peace), Sarvodaya-Patra (the pot where every household gives daily handful of grain) and Jeevandan (Gift of Life). Jayprakash Narayan, in 1954, gave the gift of his life. Vinoba acknowledged it by giving the gift of his life.

Vinoba knew the strength of the Padayatra (march on foot). He walked for 13 years throughout India. He left Paunar on September 12, 1951, and returned on April 10, 1964. He started his Toofan Yatra (journey with the speed of high-velocity wind), using a vehicle, in Bihar, in July 1965, which lasted for almost four years. He covered thousands of miles, addressed thousands of meetings and mobilised the people cutting the barriers of caste, class, language and religion. Some dacoits, from the notorious Chambal Valley (a hideout of dacoits in the northern India), surrendered themselves to Vinoba in May 1960. For Vinoba, it was a victory of nonviolence.

CHAPTER 9
Apostle of non-violence

On June 7, 1966, 50 years after his meeting with Gandhiji, Vinoba announced that he was feeling a strong urge to free himself from outer visible activities and enter inward hidden form of spiritual action. After travelling through India, he returned to Paunar on November 2, 1969, and on October 7, 1970, he announced his decision to stay at one place. He observed a year of silence from December 25, 1974 to December 25, 1975. In 1976, he undertook a fast to stop the slaughter of cows. His spiritual pursuits intensified as he withdrew from the activities.

He breathed last on November 15, 1982 at his ashram at Paunar, near Wardha.

Vinoba's contribution to the history of non-violent movement remains significant. It has to be admitted, however, that the achievement of Bhoodan or Gramdan movemen in the material terms was much below the expected target. But it has to be noted that Vinoba's movement rekindled faith in non-violence and human values advocated by Gandhiji. It presented an alternative to violence and a vision of non-violent society.

By the mid-1970s, however, the movement had begun to founder against the limits of its Utopian promise. Much of the donated land was unusable. In other cases, landowners reneged on their promises. The structures of poverty and oppression were deeper than could be reached entirely through Vinoba's appeal to love for neighbour. But, Vinoba resolutely refused to combine his moral appeal with a campaign of active resistance. In this, it was commonly observed, Vinoba differed from the Mahatma.

In later years, Vinoba devoted himself more exclusively to prayer, disillusioned by the divisiveness and rancour that had entered into the Gandhian movement itself.

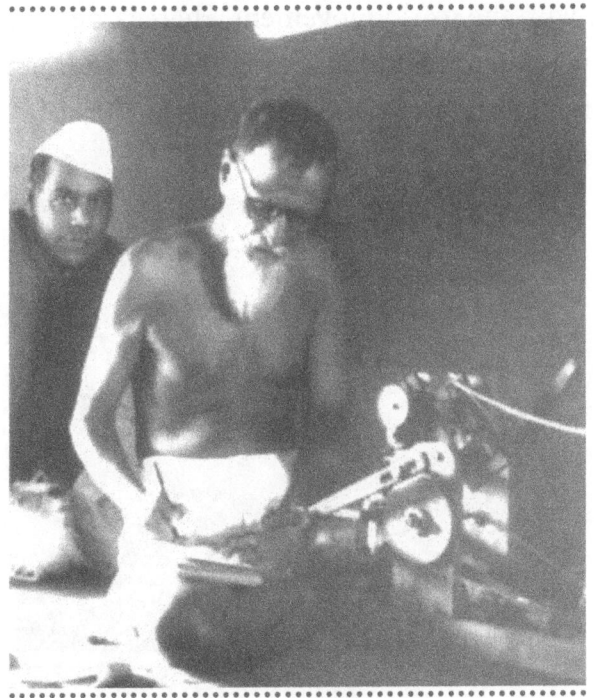

Measured against the goal of ending poverty, his movement must ultimately be judged as a heroic but failed experiment. Vinoba, however, was not so much a social activist as a man of prayer and a poet of deeds. Through the power of his personal faith, he unlocked the consciences of countless persons, and so provided a glimpse of what it would look like if a society was organised around the systematic appeal to human goodness and solidarity, rather than the narrow instincts for self-preservation and greed.

It raised important questions regarding inequality prevalent the society. Vinoba saw the land as one of the gifts of God, like air, water, sky and sunshine. He connected Science with spirituality and the autonomous village with the world movement. He regarded the power of the people superior than power of the state. Many of his ideas remain relevant and inspiring in the strife-ridden modern times.

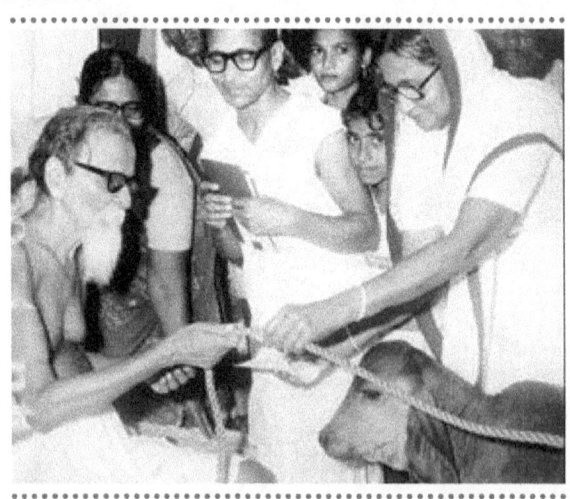

CHAPTER 10
The Padayatra

Vinoba was famous for the Padayatra, which he and his followers undertook during the Bhoodan movement. The following is an account of the foot journey by one of his associates in the historic journey.

"The pattern of Vinoba's day was daily the same. Vinoba and his company would rise by 3:00 a.m. and hold a prayer meeting for themselves. Then they would walk

ten or twelve miles to the next village, Vinoba leading at a pace that left the others struggling breathlessly behind. With him were always a few close assistants, a crowd of young, idealistic volunteers—teenagers and young adults, males and some females, mostly from towns or cities—plus maybe some regular Sarvodaya workers, a landlord, a politician, or an interested Westerner.

At the host village, a brass band, a makeshift archway, garlands, formal welcomes by village leaders, and shouts of 'Saint Vinoba, Saint Vinoba', would greet them."

"After breakfast, the Bhoodan workers would fan out through the village, meeting the villagers, distributing literature, and taking pledges. Vinoba himself would be settled apart, meeting visitors, reading newspapers, answering letters.

In late afternoon, there would be a prayer meeting, attended by hundreds or thousands of villagers from the area. After a period of reciting and chanting, Vinoba would speak to the crowd in his quiet, high-pitched voice. His talk would be completely improvised, full of rich images drawn from the Hindu scripture or everyday life, insisting the villagers to lives of love, kinship, sharing. At the close of the meeting, more pledges would be taken.

There were no free weekends on his itinerary, no holidays. The man who led this relentless crusade was 57 years old, suffered from chronic dysentery, chronic malaria, and an intestinal ulcer, and restricted himself, because of his ulcer, to a diet of honey, milk, and yoghurt."

As the campaign gained momentum, friends and detractors alike watched in fascination. In the West, too, Vinoba's effort drew attention. In the United States, major articles on Vinoba appeared in the New York Times, and the New Yorker. Vinoba even appeared on the cover of Time.

CHAPTER 11
On Gita

Of all the books by Vinoba Bhave, his talks on the Gita have been the best. An introduction to this book, in his own words, are as under,

"The Talks put the essence of the Gita into simple language and so bring it within the reach of the common man. They present the Gita from the standpoint of Samyayoga, so far as I have understood it. In the course of time my other services to the world may be forgotten, but I believe that Talks on the Gita will continue to give service. I say this because when I gave the Talks on the Gita, I did so in a state of Samadhi, in that state of consciousness, which transcends the worlds".

Talks on Gita or (Gita-Pravachane) is a very lucid and logical interpretation of Gita, with remarkable precision. It is a record of talks (Pravachans) Vinoba gave to jail inmates in Dhule, from February 1932 to June 1932, on every Sunday. It was taken down verbatim by Sane Guruji. It has a very remarkable, directly appealing and simple style of its own. The most important concept Vinoba expounds in it is pure action (Akanna), which is his personal contribution.

His own explanation of this concept is as under, "When I was studying the meaning of the Gita, it took me several years to absorb the fifth chapter. I consider that chapter to be the key to the whole book, and the key to that chapter is in the eighteenth verse of the fourth chapter, 'inaction in action, and action in inaction'. The meaning of those words, as it revealed itself to me, casts its shadow over the whole of my talks on the Gita."

Vinoba gave a running commentary on all the 18 chapters of Gita, but chose a different interpretation. Thread of discussion starts from Frustration -a means to spiritual growth, Non-conventional definition of Performance of duty (Swadhanna), Skill of Action - (Karmayoga),

Inward effort - basic parameter of Karmayoga, Action without activity - Akarma, One-pointedness of mind – Akagratha, Devotion (Bhakti) - Redefined, Pure state of mind - Samskar Mukti, Self-surrender - Basis of spiritual experience, Looking for God, The Vision of the Cosmic Form, Devotion with and without form, The Self and the Non-self, Building up and Breaking down, Completeness of Vision, Conflict Between Divine And Demonic Tendencies, Programme for the Seeker, and finally ends with Grace of the Lord.

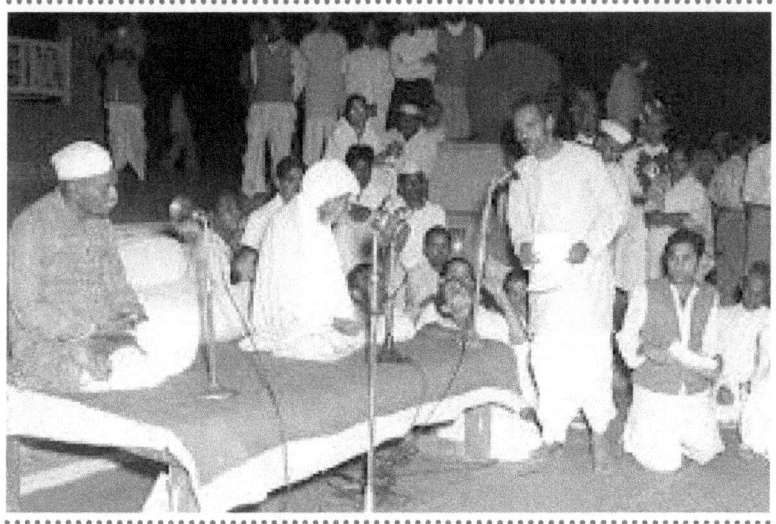

As mentioned earlier, these talks on Gita were given once a week in the prison at Dhule, one of the eastern districts in the state of Maharashtra, where Vinoba was a political prisoner. Vinoba was under a strong Gandhian influence and, hence, he worked out a different interpretation of this sacred text in line with the freedom movement that was in full swing at that time.

Although there are number of commentaries on Gita by distinguished scholars from India and abroad, Vinoba did not write such commentary. His talks on Gita in Jail, taken down verbatim by his jail inmate Sane Guruji, were found so useful that printed version, originally in Marathi, was widely appreciated in his home state, and the popularity of the Marathi version attracted people from other Indian states to translate this book in their own languages.

CHAPTER 12
On education

Vinoba's views on education reflect his dissatisfaction with the prevalent system of education in his times. They are as follows.

Defects of the present education system

"At present, mistakes are being made in the field of education in two ways. First, millions of people do not get education, and, secondly, those who get it do not receive the right type of education.

The present education is concerned only with two faculties - power of memory and capacity for arguments. There are several other faculties important than these, but the present education pays no attention towards their developments.

Considering the needs of the country, this education is of no use. The state of affairs is that a boy starting from the age of six, continues to study till the age of twenty or twenty-one, and for these fifteen years, he does no work or labour. He comes out of the school without any preparation for practical living."

The task before education

"There is no true joy for the man whose life is cut off from the heavens above and the world of nature around. This means that the task before education is to change the whole system of values and the way of life that is current in our cities. How this is to be done is not a question for you and me alone, but for the whole humanity."

Tests of education

"Self-control, fearlessness and independence of thinking, these are three tests of education. Only that country is educated where these three qualities find expression."

Government and education

"But nowadays what is happening is that governments, both in our country and elsewhere, are doing their utmost to keep students under their thumb and impose upon them the ideas upon which the governments themselves are based. If the government is communist, communist ideas are instilled. If Fascists were to take over, they would all be taught Fascism. Each and every government tries to mould the minds of students according to its own brand of thought.

This, in sober truth, is a great danger to democracy.

I am personally of the view that just as judiciary is independent and the government has no authority over it, similarly the education department should be free and independent."

Acharyakul (Intellectuals organisation)

"There is nothing new in what I am going to say. I put six programmes before you,

Make the Acharyakul organisation, as it ought to be. Acharyakul stands for fearlessness, non-maliciousness and non-partisanship. Form a strong organisation of this type in every village. If it has a school, there must be teachers, and then there should be an Acharyakul.

Organize Shanti Sena. All, men and women, present here should be fully prepared to join it. If an adversary comes to kill, they should not run away but bare their chests before him and suffer everything cheerfully.

Get Sarvodaya Patra maintained in every home. The work of getting cow slaughter banned should be carried on throughout the country.

Padayatras should be organised. As Pundit Madan Mohan Malaviyaji once said, "Meetings should be held in every village; inspiring stories should be narrated in every village; schools should also be places of physical exercise; and there should be Gosadans (cow homes) in every village." Select a village and take up integrated work there. It will have an impact on other districts and on the whole country. In addition to these, also propagate Nagari as a world script.

It is the work of the police to establish law and order through repression; it is the function of the Acharyas to establish peace through pacification and reconciliation."

> "It is only when our life proceeds within bounds and in an accepted, disciplined way, that the mind can be free."
>
> *Vinoba Bhave*

CHAPTER 13
On Hinduism

Vinoba Bhave's thoughts on religion, especially Hindu religion, show his egalitarian spirit for all religions of the world. Below are a few excerpts of his views on religion:

Hinduism, no narrowness

"Hinduism gives its followers complete freedom. It does not insist on any particular discipline or prayer. Religion has to release us from bondage. The only imperative commandment it can have is to ask us to purify ourselves. Hinduism has emphasized the need for inner purity. Indian civilization and culture has shown a tremendous capacity for assimilation and absorption. If Hinduism becomes narrow, we shall be destroying our precious heritage."

Hinduism not exclusive

"In fact, I do not find any difference in the various religions - Hinduism, Islam, Christianity, Buddhism etc. Having grown up in different countries, their outward forms are different, but in essence they are the same. So my Hinduism is not exclusive. It includes every other religion.

Though my roots are in Hinduism, yet I have studied the Bible, with as great a respect as the Gita. Likewise, I have studied the Koran. The Sermon on the Mount satisfies me as much as the Gita. Thus my environment seems to be Hindu but there is no Hinduism in it."

Gautam Buddha, a Hindu reformer

"He (Gautam Buddha) was a greater reformer of Hinduism. He was a Hindu and died a Hindu. That is my belief. Our society recognized it by accepting him as an incarnation.

The ideas of the Buddha are attracting the whole world today. The world needs them. Their attractions are their rationalism, attack on casteism, renunciation, compassion, non-enmity etc. Among these, I assign chief place to compassion and non-enmity.

The message, which Lord Buddha delivered to the world was fashioned by him and it notes a result of any speculative thinking but out of his experiences of life. It has stood the test of centuries and shines even brighter today than ever before.

What is that message?

Not by hatred is hatred appeased; not by anger is anger pacified; not by falsehood is falsehood eradicated. Hatred will only inflame hatred, and anger aggravates anger. Hatred must therefore be met by love, anger by peace, and falsehood by truth."

Buddha's message is not new. But the ways of the world have remained more or less unchanged. Because, while the people respected him whoever attained this ideal, they did not consider it worth acting upon in practical life. There was another reason why this message did not spread among the masses. Because hatred is not likely to disappear as long the factors, which excite it, are existent."

CHAPTER 14
On Peace

The following are the comments of Vinoba Bhave, the advocate of non-violence and peace.

Meaning of peace

"These days absence of war is regarded as peace. But peace really connotes absence of fear. There would be peace only when no part of the world is afraid of or exploited by any other part.

What is needed for peace is a constructive approach. Peace is something mental and spiritual. If there be peace in our (personal) life, it will affect the whole world."

Peace and armaments

"It is a delusion that only when all nations are armed and strong, will there be peace among them. Efforts to establish non-violence through violence have failed innumerable times, and they shall not only fail in future too but shall also make the whole humanity unsuccessful.

Non-violent resistance to war is final result of a non-violent attitude and not the first, as many Western pacifists seem to think."

Military power and strength

"It is wrong to think that a country's strength lies in its military power only. A nation will become really strong only if it is free from internal conflicts, if it becomes self-sufficient and the people within are united by bonds of love. If we make our country strong like this, whatever be the threats or dangers that may confront us, none of them will cast any shadow on us. On the other hand, our greatness will certainly have a good influence on outside world.

A country will have to be defended not by arms but by fearlessness, ethical behaviour and unity."

India and disarmament

"Some courage, imagination and faith are needed for disarmament, and I will say, India can certainly come

forward in unilateral disarmament because of its great tradition. So also other countries of the world because of their own particular situations. As regards unilateral disarmament, I have as much hope from England as from India."

Attitude towards war

"If we look only to the outward form of nonviolence, it will not be found to be potent enough. Hence I do not want to waste my energy in resistance to outward symbols of non-violence. I find great solace and much strength in the phrase of scripture, 'Resist not Evil'. It does not say resist evil in a non-violent way. The attempt to resist violence outwardly will only prolong its evil. When light shines, it dispels darkness. There is no resistance between light and darkness. Darkness merely vanishes. Those who believe in the power of love, non-violence and compassion should reiterate their full faith and try to persuade for right thinking.

As regards helping war-efforts, I said humorously that by walking I am doing both -supporting and opposing war-efforts. If you like, I am helping war-effort in that I am freeing the railway and other transports for military movement. I place also no impediment. Thus I am helping war-effort. Or, if you like by not buying a ticket and refusing to use the railway, I am not giving a single penny for war and thus I am opposing the war-effort.

The main thing is that people should not go mad, lose perspective and their sense of proportion.

Sometimes cold war is far worse than war itself. There is a 'cold war' and also a 'hot peace'. One thing that we must appreciate about India is that the whole nation was forcibly disarmed under the British regime. Hence there is a sort of inferiority complex among the educated people.

We should find out ways of abolishing war, but even then if they continue and we have to go render aid to the wounded soldiers, we should do it. We should not refuse it on the ground that it is a part of war, but we must keep it in mind that it is not our real work."

Essential conditions for internal peace

"If status quo continues, if the poor in the villages are neglected and if disparities go on aggravating, no force will be able to check internal disorder and external aggression.

For peace and security within the country, we must cast off mutual differences and share our weal and woe together. Sharing decreases misery and increases joy."

CHAPTER 15
On the Deed of Shanti Sena

For the re-establishment of the war-ridden world of today, Vinoba Bhave advocated the formation of a Shanti Sena. Various aspects of the Shanti Sena, according to Bhave, are given below:

The birth of Shanti Sena

"The Shanti Sena is not a new proposal. We owe both the word and the idea behind it to Bapu, who himself endeavoured to give it a practical shape. He was both its commander and its first soldier. As commander he issued the order, 'Do or Die', as a soldier he obeyed it. That is, his life and actions give us a complete picture of what the Shanti Sena is. No doubt, he also expounded his ideas freely in words, but it was through action, through life, that his thought was most fully expressed.

The functions of Shanti Sena

The Shanti Sena is an army, which offers its services in perpetuity to all men without distinction. A sick man is given the same care, no matter what is his caste, his religion or his politics, and no matter whether he lives nobly or wickedly. All that matters is that he is a man in need. We have therefore to set up this sort of army which will serve the needs impartially, disinterestedly, without asking for any reward. Its whole vocation will be to confront hatred and love."

Qualifications of a Shanti Sainik

"A member of Shanti Sena, whether a man or a woman, must have a living faith in non-violence. This is only possible if one has a living faith in God. Without that, one would not have the courage to lay down one's life without anger, fear and desire for vengeance.

This messenger of peace should have equal respect

for all the prominent religions of the world. If he were a Hindu, he would have equal reverence for other religions found in India. He should have the knowledge of the principles common to various religions.

It need not be mentioned that one who works for peace should have a blameless character. He should be reputed for his impartiality."

The pledge of a Shanti Sainik

"The main principle of Shanti Sena is that they should be free from partisanship, free from hatred, free from fear. They will trust one another, will fear none, and will frighten none. They will consider no man their enemy; their hearts will be filled with love. This is the pledge of the Shanti Sainik."

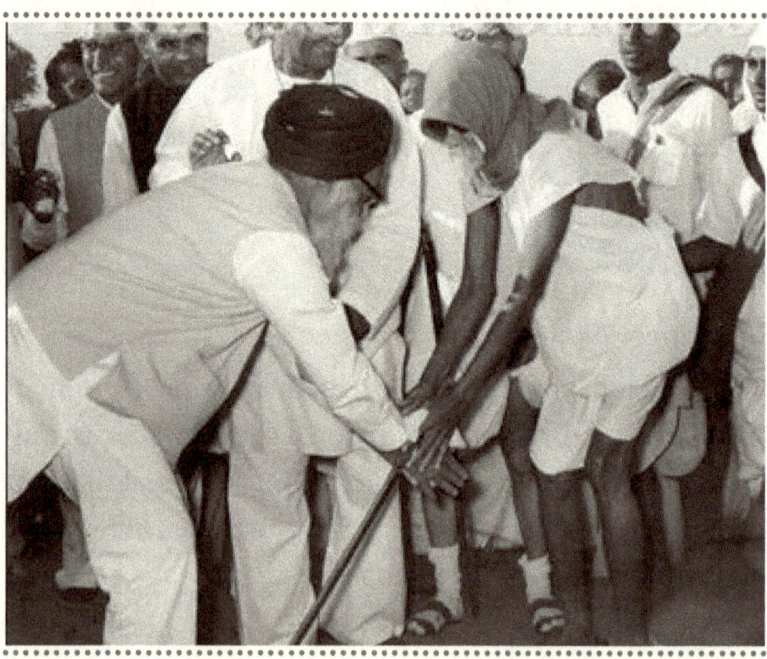

"Some portion of the primary training of the army is also essential for Shanti Sena. It is about discipline, drill, chorus singing, etc. A volunteer should know how to remove the wounded. He should have such articles with him as are need for First Aid. He should know how to extinguish fire, how to enter safely a place on fire, how to climb up with or without a load and to descend safely."

Women and Shanti Sena

"If women will take up the work of Shanti Sena, the face of the world will change, and we shall be able to achieve freedom from the problems, which we are facing today in the country and abroad. Men cannot do all this. They are not in their proper senses. They cannot think out of it. The only solution they can find is to increase armaments. Thus in this age of science, when men's brains have become paralysed, if our women come forward with their divine qualities of restraint and modesty, and use their mother-power, they can establish the rule of compassion.

In the path of violence, men will always lead. But in the part of non-violence, women can go ahead of them. So it is essential that women should lead, and that too in their own way. The way of women is the way of compassion."

Shanti Sena and War

"It will be the Shanti Sena's task to remove the root causes of unrest - the gulf between the haves and the have-nots, the pride of ownership, the insistence of 'mine' and 'thine', on high and low, on caste distinction, on religious differences and disputes. These are all causes of unrest, some economic, some social, some religious. The Shanti Sena will, therefore, be a full-time service army, working to remove these causes of dissensions and to find peaceful solutions to national problems. The result will be a cleansing of the national mind and growth of mutual goodwill. When that takes place, the government will not have to spend much on the army; the moral strength of the nation will be increased and it will be able to make its influence felt in the international field.

The full time friendly service, which it renders, will make it respected both at home and abroad."

Essentials for a Shanti Sainik
- Faith in Truth and Non-violence.
- A fearless, non-malicious and non-party attitude.
- Making no distinctions on the basis of country, creed, race, caste, language, etc.
- Standing fully aloof from power and party politics. No support to war preparedness to undertake even risk to life in calming disorders observance of the Shanti Sena discipline.

CHAPTER 16
On Cow Slaughter and Vegetarianism

Vinoba Bhave was one of the staunch opponent of cow slaughter and advocated for the protection of cows. Below are his views on Cow protection and vegetarianism:

Cow protection

"Protection of the cow and the bullock is a characteristic of the Indian social philosophy. We are, in this respect, a step ahead of the Western socialism. Western socialism asks for a full and equal protection being given to all men,

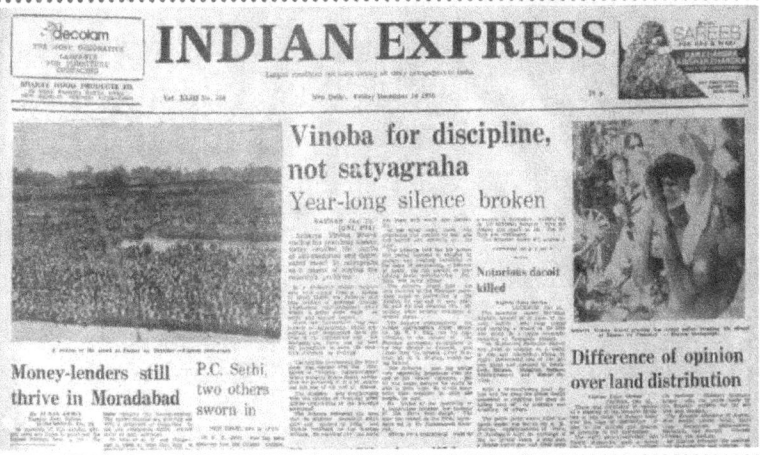

but there it stops. We in India have gone a step further. We have included the cow as a member in the family. True, we have not followed this principle in practice fully. We merely pay respect to the cow but do not look after it so well as they do in the Western countries. Nevertheless we have deep regard for it and consider it worthy of our care and protection in the same way as the human members of the family. We do not drive out the latter when they grow old. In the same way, though we make full use of the cow and the bullock - take milk, get our fields ploughed, use the dung for manure, and use even their hides after they are dead - we do not kill them. But now we must link up this regard with a scientific attitude.

Superstitious respect will not do. We must open good dairy farms, Gosadans, and the wealthy amongst us should come forward to provide for the upkeep of decrepit cattle."

Ban on cow slaughter

"Some people are under serious misapprehension in regard to the secular character of our State. They think that there is some kind of incompatibility between cow protection and a secular State. There is no incompatibility between the secular character of our State and the protection of the cow. No religion in India says that it is meritorious to kill a cow, and therefore there is no conflict among our different religions about the desirability of the protection of the cow. Therefore I say that there is nothing to prevent secular State from striving to protect the cow, and our State must do it."

Vegetarianism

"I believe that India's special contribution to the history of non-violence is the giving up of animal food. Not that all Indians are vegetarians, but the idea commands the respect of all. I have seen many a cruel person among habitual vegetarians and many a kind one among meat eaters. In spite of this, I believe that vegetarianism will go a long way to help the evolution of non-violence, and humanity will be imperfect without it."

"With me it is also an article of faith that the modern man has got to attain, sooner rather than later, an adult status, when he shall kill no creature of God for food or sport, when he will refuse to lock upon any living being as his food. For, mankind must reach the conclusion soon enough that vegetarian food is the best food for man so as to enable him to outgrow the beast in him. I am also aware that enough vegetarian food is not available in the world today. Nevertheless, I submit that the reform is essential for the evolution and perfection of man and for the unity of religious and spiritual endeavour of all mankind."

CHAPTER 17
Concept of Modern Society

Vinoba Bhave's concept of modern society reveals the man in him, who has aptly been called the 'king of kindness'. He believed that movements like Bhoodan and sampattidan can contribute a great deal towards the formation of a modern Indian society. Below is an excerpt of his views on the modern society:

"We should do things first to bring about unity between men of different religions and languages, and remove the chasm between the rich and poor.

The Bhoodan movement is no one-sided affair confined to just one sector of our economic life. It includes all efforts aimed at building up a strong and noble life throughout our land. It certainly includes moral regeneration of our people. The redistribution of land and promotion of village industries will help in eradicating poverty and clear the way for moral uplift.

Bhoodan wants and love to become the dominant values in society. All problems ought to be solved by negotiations in a spirit of friendliness.

We seek to reconstruct society on a new basis. That is the purpose behind the Bhoodan work. The Bhoodan movement is for us an instrument for achieving a non-violent and peaceful change of values."

Sampattidan (wealth gift)

"From Bhoodan, Sampattidan was a natural step, and the idea that along with Bhoodan I should also ask for Sampattidan, did occur to me and held my mind. But the land problem was a basic one and I saw that unless something was done to meet it, it might develop into a big danger detrimental to the security of the nation. I, therefore, thought it fit first to concentrate my energy only on that question.

But as the work of the Bhoodan progressed, it became increasingly clear that the idea behind the movement could not be fulfilled unless we went further and asked for a portion of wealth and property. The idea behind the demand is that all wealth, even though we may acquire it with our individual effort and skill, is not for us alone, but has been granted to by God for all of us."

Gramdan(village-gift)

"Gramdan is an expression of the spirit of the age. It asks people not only to break the narrow domestic walls and consider the whole village as one family, but goes further and asks all villagers to meet together to consider their common problems and to solve them with one mind.

Gramdan symbolizes human compassion. Gramdan has a dual objective of before it, namely, to wipe out social disparities and to reduce economic inequalities."

Sarvodaya Patra

"In Sarvodaya-patra, my rule is that only children should put in it a handful of grain. Its main aim is to give training to children and to obtain a pledge from every family that they would not take part in anything that disturbs peace."

CHAPTER 18
On Planning

There is no end to Vinoba's thoughts for the uplift of the poor, the depressed and the down trodden of the nation. Following are his views on planning:

The fundamental principles of planning

"It should be a postulate of national planning that at present all can and should be provided full employment. Let them do it with such tools and machineries as are capable of it. However, if only some can be provided work on the plea of efficiency, it would not be national but partial planning.

The government plans ought to give the first priority to the raising up of the lowest, the poorest and the most depressed.

Planning must primarily mean employment and food to everyone. They talk of raising the standard of living. No one would object to it, if could be done, but before we talk of increasing the standard of living, we have to assure ourselves that we shall first live. Let us first assure, minimum livelihood to all.

A society based on non-violence cannot function through intermediate agencies. To bring about such a society, village industries should thrive. All should get food and all must work. The economy of the nation should be planned on the lines of a joint family."

Decentralisation of planning

"The method of Baba's (Vinoba's) planning is different from that adopted in the present plans. Their method is that of nationalised planning, i.e. the plan for the whole of the country is drawn up in Delhi. Baba wants every village to prepare its own plan".

Small schemes

"If we plan and work out small schemes with our own resources and capacity, the progress of the country would be greater than it would be if we burden ourselves with big schemes. We can perform big tasks, but they would not be done till we acquire skill in performing small ones."

CHAPTER 19
Vinoba's Message

Vinoba, when soon after Gandhi's death was asked how Gandhians should go about setting up peace brigades, replied that the units had to be formed on a local basis without an India-wide central organisation. In answering the question about how to commence the work, he responded,

"The work gets done once it is begun. Make a very natural beginning. Take a day off in a week and go out as if for an excursion. Go to a village alone, or with friends and members of your family five or six kilometres away. Take your food with you for the day.... Mix with the people there, make friends with them. Interest yourself in their joys and sorrows. In this way make your acquaintance with a few villages in the neighbourhood one after another, and then repeat the cycle. The time would soon arrive when the village folk will learn to look on you as their friend who does not make any demand on them other than that of love and cooperation. Moving among the people is the initial stage of the programme before Shanti Sena. The rest will follow automatically."

Brahmavidya Mandir

"Brahmavidya Mandir is an ashram in the middle of India, originally set up by Vinoba Bhave. Vinoba was a follower of Gandhi, and a spiritual freedom fighter in his own right. The ashram is situated on the banks of the River Dham, some 10 km from Wardha, in the centre of India. Vinoba first came to this spot in 1938 to take rest from his activities at that time, and it was here that some of his spiritual-social experiments took place. Basically, the idea was to have a place where people could live and lead a spiritual existence in a way different from many other ashrams, in that it involved being fully self-sufficient and that it was mainly inhabited by women. The basic principles followed in the ashram are based on Gandhi's 11 vows for living. These are non-violence, truth, non-stealing, chastity, non-possession, manual labour, control of palate, complete fearlessness, equality of religions, using native country goods and removal of untouchability. The aim was to create a community that upheld these vows and led a spiritually contemplative life for the benefit of themselves and society in general. Now, there are 31 sisters and 4 brothers living at the ashram. This ashram is self-sufficient and do not have to rely too much on products from outside. The ashram has now some difficulties to keep on the agricultural work due to the fact that over half the inhabitants of the ashram are now over 70 years of age, and have some physical restrictions. This is ashram life-simple, orderly, disciplined and contemplative."

CHAPTER 20
On Political System

Following are Vinoba's views on the political system during his time:

"What goes on the villages, where every man manages his own life, is real self-government... It follows that we shall have swaraj when all the people have acquired the strength of self-control and have realized their duties. Until then, we shall only have government."

The very institutions and procedures that one refers to when he speaks of India's democracy, namely the government, the elections, and the politicians, all prevent him from achieving real democratic living. In a compilation of essays, entitled Democratic Values, prevalent Vinoba Bhave clearly captured how the form of government people have destroyed their senses of independence, unity, justice, freedom, creativity, and ultimately their ability to develop real Swaraj. He argued that unless people liberate themselves from formal political procedures institutions, and develop more just and nurturing interactions amongst themselves, they cannot hope to live democratically. The following is an excerpt from Vinoba's Democratic Values:

Our 'Democracy' Fosters Dependency

Government is a state of slavery. One of the biggest plights today is our dependency on government. We expect it to protect us, feed us, employ us, etc. But by waiting for the government to fulfill our every need and to solve all of our problems, by 'invoking the government as though it were God,' we become its slaves.

In this way, government is also a disease. It makes people feel insecure or incompetent, as though they can do nothing without it and do nothing in its presence. This feeling of powerlessness is carried further by our system of elections and political parties, where only people with wealth, property, or party support can afford to stand for elections. Not only does this criterion eliminate the voices of huge portions of the population, but it also perpetuates injustice by forcing us to place our lives in the hands of an insensitive elite.

Our political actions are limited to either casting a vote or soliciting votes. But managing our affairs by voting will not bring about the socio-spiritual revolutions we need today. Voting does not capture our energy, ideas or potential, nor does it allow us to think creatively about the future or about new directions for change. Majority rule, 'winner-take-all' political structures, do not provide the opportunity to build consensus and cooperation on issues of significance, while the role of the 'opposition' has been reduced to 'destabilising' the ruling party and grabbing power. Without spaces for constructive dialogue, reflection, and building new relationships, all we are left with is empty political posturing, increased disillusionment, and greater suffering for all.

Our 'Democracy' Prevents Real Swaraj

Today, in mainstream society, power is equated with 'might is right' — fear, domination, threat, and control. In contrast, Vinoba defined true Swaraj from two perspectives: "no outside power exercises control over you and you do not exercise power over anyone else." In this way, Swaraj permits neither submission nor exploitation. Such a vision seeks to push us beyond dehumanising categories of 'oppressed' or 'oppressor'. Simultaneously, it extends the notion of power beyond state and market systems to restore agency/power/moral conscience to every human being. In our current political system, 'no one tells you the real truth — that your destiny, heaven or hell, is in your own hands, and that no one but yourself can take you there.'

Vinoba believed that "revolutions are never achieved by power or party politics. Revolutions, and thus real Swaraj, take place in the minds of people. The fact is, representative politics has led India into deep intellectual, cultural, and spiritual stagnation. Real Swaraj requires that people transcend party lines and open their hearts to ideas and to each other. Going beyond partisanship politics also requires that we recognize and explore other spaces of power and opportunities for decision-making to expand our sense of social and civic commitment."

CHAPTER 21
An Anecdote

Through his exemplary life, Vinoba Bhave influenced many people around him, and many came for his advice. The following is an interesting anecdote of how he changed the lives of his fellowmen in a noble way.

Once, a woman came to see Vinoba Bhave and said, "I am very unhappy."

Vinoba asked, "What is the matter?" In a voice foil of grief, she replied, "My husband is an alcoholic. He drinks everyday and abuses me. Sometimes, he beats me up. My life is hell."

Vinoba asked, "When he gets drunk, what do you do?"

She replied, "I get upset. Earlier, I used to scold him. That did not help. So now I have started to observe fasts."

"You do not eat or drink during the fast?," asked Vinoba.

"No," she said, "I eat fruit."

Vinoba said in a simple natural tone, "Oh, then your husband must get very upset. Your eating fruits must have increased the household expenses."

The woman kept quiet. Tears filled her eyes. Vinoba said, "Nobody can be made to give up wrong things by our getting angry or by our giving up food. We can change others through love and patience. The love that can make the difference comes from within. Our hearts should be pure. If there are bad feelings in our hearts and we show insincere love, it makes matters worse."

The woman asked, "What should I do? I lose control of my senses when I see him drunk."

"This is the root cause of your trouble," explained Vinoba. He continued, "You can bring your husband back from the path of evil only when you control your own bad feelings. First you should try to change yourself."

The woman bowed and left. The joy of having found a noble way reflected on her face.

CHAPTER 22
Contemporaries of Vinoba

Gandhiji appointed Vinoba as his 'spiritual heir', and Pandit Nehru as 'Political heir'. Many times Vinoba remarked, "We are disciple-brother."

Jawaharlal Nehru, the first Prime minister of India, shared a very warm relationship with Vinoba. In fact, he even discussed many national and international issues with him. When Vinoba said frankly in public that India should resort to unilateral disarmament for the sake of world peace, he thought that it might be embarrassing to Nehru, so he sent for a messenger to ask Nehru if that was so, who replied that Vinoba should freely say whatever he thought was appropriate. Nehru called Vinoba 'a philosopher king'.

When Indira Gandhi became the Prime Minister, Vinoba said, "Nehru was a great man. Prime Minister was a small thing in relation to him and because he was so great, he might not perhaps succeeded as a Prime Minister. His daughter would me more successful as a Prime minister." To the question as to why if he loved Nehru so much, he did not help in elections, Vinoba said, "Yes, I love him very much. I would even give up my life for him, but I will not give my vote."

He was one of those people who rendered his service to the nation, and yet remained aloof from the politics. Vinoba never voted in any elections.

Apart from the Nehrus and the Gandhis, Vinoba shared cordial relations with other contemporary leaders of his times, as well. When Lal Bahadur Shastri became the Prime Minister after Nehru, he went to village Jamani, near Wardha, to obtain Vinoba's blessings, and to cope up with the new responsibility.

India's first President, Dr. Rajendra Prasad, and Vinoba shared a very close relationship. He often visited Vinoba and attended Sarvodaya get-together. Vinoba frequently said, "Rajendrababu is physically in Rashtrapati Bhavan, but his mind is in villages." Rajendrababu kept a 'Sarvodaya receptacle' in Rashtrapati Bhavan. Vinoba referred to it time and again and said, "Violence dictates, non-violence insinuates. The President himself having installed a 'Sarvodaya receptacle', every citizen ought to do the same."

India's third President, Dr. Zakir Husain, worked for 'basic education' under Gandhiji's guidance. Because of this, he had a close relationship with Vinoba for many years. The two often discussed for hours together how to revolutionize education.

After becoming the President, Dr. Zakir Husain met Vinoba, and the latter said, "What a fine coincidence. After one teacher (Radha Krishanan) went, there comes another." Hearing this, Zakir Husain bowed in humility and said, "Yes, but the one who went was a very great man; the one who came in is very small man." Vinoba told this story many times and always said that Zakir saheb's humility had a great influence on him.

Every Prime Minister of India called on Vinoba, but Indira Gandhi met him on more occasions than the others. In fact, after she became the Prime Minister, Vinoba initiated her into spiritual studies. Though he extended paternal love to Indira Gandhi, Vinoba did not hesitate to rebuke her as well. Time and again, he warned her that the emergency should not be prolonged beyond six months as that would be damaging. He also advised her to go for elections in 1976, which would bring her great success. He was much pleased that a woman became a Prime Minister.

CHAPTER 23
Jayprakash Narayan on Vinoba

Jayprakash Narayan, the 'Loknayak of India', dedicated his life (Jeevandaan) to Vinoba Bhave's Sarvodaya movement. Below is an excerpt of his writings on Vinoba Bhave.

During Gandhi's life Vinoba's name was not much known even in India. Today, however, the remotest villages resound with the words 'Vinoba' and Bhoodan. Even outside India, well-informed cycles have been set up to take notice of the 'walking saint' and his land gift mission. Many thinkers in the West have seen in Vinoba's message a solvent for the war of ideologies that has become the despair of the human race.

"I shall not forget the occasion when the Rev. Dr. Martin Luther King, the leader of the Montgomery, Alabama, movement of non-violent resistance to racial segregation, met Vinoba with his wife. Jim Bristol of the Quaker Centre, Delhi, it was, I think, who in introducing Mrs. King spoke of her proficiency in music and suggested that she might sing somehymns and Negro spirituals for Vinoba. Everyone was delighted at the suggestion.

I looked at Vinoba and wondered if he knew what the Negro spirituals were. We were all startled, most of all the Americans, when Vinoba, as if in answer raised is ever downcast eyes towards Mrs. King and intoned softly, "Were you there, were you there, When they crucified my Lord?" When Mrs. King sang that spiritual, it had an added poignancy for us.

"Vinoba is a linguist. Besides Sanskrit, Pali and Arabic, he knows English well, reads French, was recently learning German, and knows all the major Indian languages. He loved mathematics. His quest for knowledge is insatiable. But it is not knowledge as ordinarily understood. Most knowledge he regards as superficial and is interested in seeking after the fundamental truths of life. He has an uncanny capacity for separating the chaff from the grain and going to the root of the question. I have not met another person with a keen razor-like mind as Vinoba."

From the first day of contact, Vinoba remained steadfast in his loyalty and devotion to his chosen master, though it would be doing an injustice to him to regard him as a disciple in any narrow sense of the term. It was clear to those who came to know him even during Gandhi's life time, that he possessed a mind and character, an originality and above all, a spiritual quality, that were destined to take him beyond the limits of a mere follower - no matter how brilliant - and make him a master in his own right. Those who have followed closely Vinoba's work and thought know how great have been his own experiments with truth and how significant his contributions to human thought. Particularly significant has been his development of the theory and practice of Satyagraha beyond the stage where Gandhi left them.

"It must be said that it (Bhoodan) is the first attempt in history to bring about a social revolution and reconstruction by the means of love. Vinoba is doing a path-finding job in this field. The results of his experiment may have a far-reaching impact on a world that is so torn with hatred and charged with violence."

One final word about Vinoba is essential so that he may be truly understood. Vinoba is not a politician, nor a social reformer, nor a revolutionary. He is first and last a man of God. Service of man is to him nothing but an effort to unite with God. He endeavours every second to blot himself out, to make himself empty so that God may fill him up and make him his instrument. The talks of such a man of self realization on one of the profoundest spiritual works of all times should be of inestimable value to all- irrespective of race, creed or nationality.

CHAPTER 24
Awards and Recognitions

Vinoba received the 'Mahatma Gandhi Award' for his service to the Hindi language, and the 'Magsaysay Award' for his social service. The whole world honoured and recognised the work of the 'walking saint who distributed land to the poor'. Many peacekeepers like Donald Groom of England joined his pilgrimages on foot. A majority of them were young people.

England's Poet Laureate Lord Tennyson's grandson, Hallum Tennyson, joined a Vinoba's pilgrimage for a few days and wrote a book about him, Saint on the March. Hallum Tennyson gifted his income from the book to Vinoba's work. To propagate it, he even conducted a pilgrimage on foot in England.

Lance d' Elavasta of France wrote a book in French, *From Gandhi to Vinoba*: A New Pilgrimage.

This writer, is well-known by the pen name of Shantidas, and also runs an ashram in France.

Communist leader S. A. Dange and Vinoba were acquainted since the Telangana pilgrimage days. During

Vinoba's last days, Dange specially went to Paunar to meet him. He called Vinoba 'saviour of the poor' and praised the great work of the land-donation and village-donation movement done by him.

During the pilgrimage of Vidarbha, Shri Golwalkar Guruji of Rashtriya Swayamsevak Sangh came to meet Vinoba. They had a frank discussion for two hours. Vinoba said to him, "Hinduism is like an ocean. It accommodates all within itself. Hindusim cannot tolerate narrow-mindedness." Guruji acquainted Vinoba with his work. Vinoba told him, "I have written books on the essence of all religions. Special classes should be conducted for the study of 'Essence of Koran', 'Essence of Christianity' and so on. Besides, special emphasis should be laid on rendering service to Adivasis and the oppressed, neglected poor. Swami Vivekananda has given the mantra to worship god in the poor."

After the pilgrimage of Kashmir, Pakistan's Consul General in India, Mr. Brohi, came to meet Vinoba in a village in Punjab. He was the first Pakistani to call on him. In a public meeting he on Vinoba's birthday, said, "Vinoba is, household name in Pakistan. 'A fakir who gives land to the poor' is how our people know him."

Gandhiji's technique of non-violence, non-cooperation began to be used in many countries of the world, and they started having their own 'Gandhi'. The black leader, Martin Luther King, renowned as the Gandhi of America, came to meet Vinoba during his pilgrimage of Rajasthan. He created an extraordinary awakening among the oppressed and exploited black population of America, by showing them the new path of nonviolence. When he met Vinoba, he acquainted him with his movement and asked for his blessings. Vinoba asked him to sing Christian hymns. He told Vinoba that he got inspiration and strength by meeting him, and felt as though he had met Gandhiji himself.

www.ingramcontent.com/pod-product-compliance
Lightning Source LLC
LaVergne TN
LVHW091316080426
835510LV00007B/519